THE CHRISTIAN AND WARFARE

The Roots of Pacifism in the Old Testament

by

Jacob J. Enz

HERALD PRESS, SCOTTDALE, PENNSYLVANIA

CHRISTIAN PEACE SHELF SERIES

The Christian Peace Shelf is a series of books and pamphlets devoted to the promotion of Christian peace principles and their applications. The editor, who is appointed by the Mennonite Central Committee Peace Section, and an editorial board from the Brethren in Christ Church, General Conference Mennonite Church, Mennonite Brethren Church, and Mennonite Church, represent the historic concern for peace within these brotherhoods.

1. **Nevertheless** by John H. Yoder. 1971.
2. **Coals of Fire** by
   Elizabeth Hershberger Bauman. 1954.
3. **The Christian and Warfare** by
   Jacob J. Enz. 1972.

THE CHRISTIAN AND WARFARE
Copyright © 1972 by Herald Press, Scottdale, Pa. 15683
International Standard Book Number: 0-8361-1684-4
Printed in the United States

Preface

It is high time to set aside the BB-gun method of the proof-texting, inner-canon approach to the presentation of biblical pacifism and draw up the heavy artillery of the insights which the very substructure of biblical thought brings to bear upon a question so vital to the church, to say nothing about civilization itself. If pacifism is not found in the very fabric of biblical thought, no amount of proof-texting will be convincing. The following series of lectures has grown out of the conviction that pacifism is deeply rooted in such pervasive biblical concepts as creation, covenant, kingdom, incarnation, substitution, proclamation, and Messianic hope. The object of the lectures is not so much to formulate a biblical doctrine of pacifism as to reexamine the aforementioned biblical concepts and draw the implications they have for pacifism.

This book is the substance of the Menno Simons Lectures as originally delivered at Bethel College, North Newton, Kansas, in 1957. The lectures were prepared and delivered with a rather varied audience in mind -- college students, college faculty, and laymen.

Heartfelt gratitude is hereby expressed to the Menno Simons Lectureship Foundation of Bethel College for the opportunity to bring together the fruit of encounter in the study of Bible and biblical theology with Mennonite and Church of the Brethren seminarians at Mennonite Biblical Seminary in Chicago (as associated at that time with Bethany Biblical Seminary, graduate school of theological education of the Church of the Brethren).

Heavy indebtedness to the personal stimulation of the late W. F. Albright, Professor Emeritus of Semitic Languages and Literature at The Johns Hopkins University, is gladly acknowledged here. The influence of the writings of G. Ernest Wright (Harvard University) and Donald G. Miller is also recognized with gratitude.

Jacob J. Enz

Mennonite Biblical Seminary
Elkhart, Indiana
October 13, 1971

Contents

1 The Recovery
of the Ultimate Weapon
(The Proclamation
of the Biblical
Word-Deed of Love)

The profound audacity of the gospel is its claim to the possession of the ultimate weapon — the word-deed of love.

The painful almost impossibly stupid situation in which the church finds itself is to have in its possession the knowledge of this ultimate weapon without being much concerned about its use, much less about its sharing. The crime which the church is committing is infinitely greater than if some great clinic laboratory known the world over for its advanced research in cancer should be found the possessor of the cure for cancer for the last twenty-five years without having shared the formula with other hospitals or even applied it to cancer patients in its own wards. The gospel formula is so authenticated. The church's neglect is that catastrophic.

The value of the spoken and written word has been hit by a wave of inflation far more serious than anything our economic structures of the world are experiencing. In academic circles the trend has been reversed, but the trend first set in motion in academic circles has reached the seed-bearing stage among people in general.

We think of words as harmless little projectiles which we may send out into space with very little worry or sense of responsibility about them because they are so inconsequential, so intangible, so seemingly harmless and ineffective. In an outdated radical empiricism only that which could be measured by the senses was seriously taken into account — what we could see, hear, taste, smell, and touch. The rest, because it did not lend itself to our very inadequate means of measurement which we deliberately kept at a minimum, we simply ruled out of existence. Now it is in this realm of experience, in the deep inaccessible reaches of the personality that language and meaning arise. In the unmeasurable realms of personality words have their most profound effect. Careful students of personality and society have brought these areas back into legitimate concerns of study even if the tools for research may still lack full development and be controversial.

Primitives today, Orientals, and the ancients have a much more serious, a much healthier attitude toward words, though, to be sure, often cluttered with magic. Upon a group of potsherds turned up in Egypt called the Execration Texts, it appears quite evident that the names of a number of revolting vassals of the Egyptian empire were very carefully written. Then the pot was smashed. By breaking the name the defeat of the foe was understood as accomplished. To use the word, the name, is to possess power.

In the Bible, the promise of Isaac given to the treacherous Jacob is regarded as irretrievably given. There could be no taking back of the words spoken any more than the course of an arrow be reversed after it has left the string.

The Christian operates on this fundamental assumption — one might call it a critical dynamism — that the word is freighted with power. It is an extension of the personality of him who speaks as real as when that person reaches out and touches another. It involves him in the life of another as certainly as when he clasps the hand of another. In the realm of sex Jesus pointed this up in the Sermon on the Mount; even the look, the thought which is the mother of the word, is the equivalent of the act! Anger and contempt at the brother is a breach of the command, "Thou shalt not kill."

When we separate the word and the deed we may be following some very popular modern ways of thought, but let us be honest — we have not caught up with biblical thought. No, the Christian operates on the assumption that, far from being an impotent thing, a word expresses the inmost nature of him who speaks. It is the ultimate weapon; it is the basic energy of the universe. The word-deed is the last word in power.

Let us examine the biblical material to see how the evidence for this arises from the Bible as a whole. For any study of a given problem it is always best to start in the Gospels and Acts, the record of the mighty acts of God in Christ and the apostles and then work back to the Old Testament and forward through the epistles and Revelation. Thus we may observe the roots in the Old Testament and the fruits in the epistles and Revelation.

When we turn to the words of Jesus in what is generally regarded as the earliest Gospel, Mark, we note that He regards proclamation of the gospel as His chief task. After a day filled with various activities and a night of prayer, His disciples discovered Him and reported, apparently as a result of His mighty healing ministry of the day before, "Every one is searching for you" (Mk. 1:37). Jesus' reaction is, "Let us go on to the next towns, that I may preach there also; for that is why I came out." The following summary of His activity of "preaching . . . and casting out demons" reveals clearly that His healing ministry did not cease but paralleled and was structured by His ministry of proclamation. Since by Him the kingdom had come and since all aspects of God's creation are subservient to Him, it naturally followed that the healing ministry and the teaching ministry were involved.

When we turn to the Gospel of John, often considered the last to be written, we see that it appears to be structured by the mighty deeds of Jesus called "signs." This purposeful structuring is indicated in John 20:30, 31: "Now Jesus did many other signs in the presence of the disciples, which are not written in this book; but these are written that you may believe that Jesus is the Christ. . . ." Yet it is John alone with this singular emphasis on deeds who prefaces his Gospel by giving Jesus the name "Word"! Here and in the Book of the Revelation alone Jesus is called the "Word" (Jn. 1:1, 14; Rev. 19:13). Now the Scriptures seldom say who God is; more frequently they tell what God does. In this prominent case in John where it is told who God is, it is the name of a very real action — speaking. When John gives us his understanding of what Jesus meant to him above everything else it is *word*. It is communication. It is God reaching out in His word into the darkness of human disobedience "and the darkness has not overcome it" (Jn. 1:5).

The tremendous impact that Jesus made on John sent him searching back through the Old Testament to find a fitting parallel. He found none until he came back to the very beginning to the very first recorded activity of God when

He *spoke*, and said, "Let there be light" (Gen. 1:3). Thus he begins, "In the beginning was the Word. . . . In him was life, and the life was the light of men. The light shines in the darkness, and the darkness has not overcome it." For John nothing since the first mighty word of God is like the Word in Jesus Christ! Christ was there as well as here at Bethlehem and Calvary.

When we turn back to Genesis 1:1 we see that from the very first page of the Bible word is equated with work. Amidst the chaos at the beginning God said, "Let there be light." And there was light. The first creative act of God was accomplished by the word. This Israelite portrayal of creation is all the more significant when we recall that other accounts of creation portray it as a bloody battle of gods. One god overwhelmed by another more powerful god was cut in two. The powerful god then proceeded to make earth out of one part of the dead god and heaven out of the other. How different then: "God said . . . it was so."

Then we note that God called the light "day" and the darkness "night." To have power to give name is to possess power over another according to biblical patterns of thought. Finally, with animate creation God blesses and commands. But man stands above nature, created in the image of God. He is commanded to subdue the earth (not his fellow) and engage in the same naming activity as we had seen God perform: man was to name the animals which is the expression of man's authority over nature. In this activity man is still engaged as he employs the microscope and numerous other instruments. He seeks to determine the nature and function of various parts of creation to subdue them (as in case of disease germs, e.g.). But, painfully enough, man chooses to let nature come between him and God as in Genesis 3, and man keeps on falling.

The power of the word-deed is seen in some of the towering events in the Old Testament. Moses takes a shepherd's staff and a burning heart into Egypt and leads a band of slaves who raised not one sword against the world's greatest empire.

When Israel wanted a king to lead her in battle, God gave her a king but also prophets who poured out their lives after their words. Even now the books of Samuel and Kings are called the "Earlier Prophets" in the Hebrew Bible — not "The Monarchy"!

The writer of Hebrews describes the mighty work of Christ as our true high priest, the mediator of a better covenant (Heb. 8:6), offering once for all His own self for our sins. His stress is repeatedly on the work, the activity of Christ. However, as a title for the whole he begins this artful document by saying, "In many and various ways God spoke of old to our fathers by the prophets; but in these last days he has

13

spoken to us by a Son, whom he appointed the heir of all things, through whom also he created the world" (Heb. 1:1-3).

The Book of Revelation is soaked with free-flowing blood of judgment. Its startling portrayal gives us Christ at the beginning (1:16) and end (19:15) not with a sword at His side but a sword in His mouth. This matches the exhortation of Paul (Eph. 6:17) to the Christian to take the "sword of the Spirit, which is the word of God" in the struggle which is not against flesh and blood.

Perhaps one of the most telling instances where the word-deed is brought forth as the Christian's crucial weapon is the first chapter of Acts (1:6-8). The disciples appear still to be concerned about the establishment of a kingdom of force. "Lord, will you at this time restore the kingdom to Israel?" Jesus' answer is, "It is not for you to know times or seasons. . . . But you shall receive power when the Holy Spirit has come upon you; and you shall be my witnesses in Jerusalem and in all Judea and Samaria and to the end of the earth."

This last phrase "and to the end of the earth" reminds one of Psalm 2:8:

> Ask of me, and I will make the nations your heritage, and the ends of the earth your possession.

But note carefully how the Psalm continues:

14

You shall break them with a rod of iron,
and dash them in pieces like a potter's vessel.

Here is naked imperialism of physical force. However, in the Acts passage worldwide power is connected with "witnessing," a word taken from Isaiah (43:10, 12; 44:8) where the Servant of the Lord exercises only the power of suffering persuasion (Is. 50:5; 53). Yet we know witnessing in Acts was not word alone. It was word with the thrust of a fearless life back of it — fearlessness in service, in suffering, and in going forth on treacherous journeys to proclaim the presence of the King and the kingdom.

The motivation for this word-deed is clear. It is love. In the first chapters of Genesis the extent of love is worldwide as also in the call of Abraham and in some of the prophets. When it narrows down to a nationalistic motivation as in Psalm 2, the New Testament, in addition to Ruth and Jonah, corrects it.

The Bible then, we insist, knows only one weapon — the word-deed of love. This alone respects the total person ministering to outward needs *and* erecting sound inward faith; each ministry needs the other for "the stature of the fulness of Christ" (Eph. 4:13). The word-deed of love is the only weapon that can stab hatred, envy, and injustice because it penetrates where no bullet can — to the very motives of man.

15

This fundamental biblical perspective sounds a sharp warning for the institutional life of the church. That warning is against dividing the word ministry from the work ministry. Cliques are developed around each of them. Some give heavily to missions and neglect Christian service, schools, and literature; others specialize in the latter and neglect the former. Some missionaries look askance at relief workers; they so easily forget that the broad ministry of the whole person opens up hitherto unrecognized points of penetration for the saving Word. Some relief workers question the zeal of missionaries; they forget the lasting penetration which evangelism can give to a work ministry.

The Book of Acts sets forth the correct relation. Paul, the great missionary and preacher, brought emergency relief to the church at Jerusalem. Stephen, the first relief worker, was martyred for his powerful preaching! For the Christian forces this double strategy is as necessary as providing every soldier with food and bullets.

One of the first areas of preparation for a more effective witness of Christianity is the recovery within its own circles of the long abandoned word-deed of love. Sometimes we hear of a man without a country. A great modern hymn written during the agonies of the post-World War I period has it right:

By wars and tumults love is mocked, divided,

His conquering cross no kingdom wills to bear. . . .

The mighty word-deed of the cross presents us the greater tragedy of a flag without a country — a mighty gospel without a church.

2 Fighting in the Right War
(Decision and the Recovery of the Biblical Timetable)

The Christian life is a deep decision about time.

"In the perspective of geology and biology it is but yesterday that Moses appeared before Pharaoh to demand the release of the Israelite slave; and but a few hours more since Abraham left Ur of the Chaldees."[1] These are the words of Louis Finkelstein, president of the Jewish Theological Seminary in New York. We as Christians would then add: In the perspective of geology and biology it is but this morning that Jesus lived, taught, suffered, died, and rose again.

Finkelstein complains about certain moderns who take lightly the past of the Hebrew. He was trying to help a serious young Jew to be faithful to the law of the Sabbath. This fellow had been scheduled for an exam on Saturday, the Jewish day of rest. In taking up the matter for the boy with the official of the school, Finkelstein got this tart reply, "You don't expect us to make our rules fit those ancient regulations from the wilderness, do you?"

For a host of modern people this is either the expressed or implicit objection to the gospel and particularly, of course, to the demands of the gospel that run counter to so-called modern life. "Do you mean to tell me that what happened 2,000 years ago has a bearing on my decision today? Do you want me to believe that what Jesus said 2,000 years ago is something I have to follow tomorrow when the government asks me to register for military service? Don't be silly!"

For some moderns who are seriously challenged by Jesus on the one hand but are caught in this modern cult, the problem turns up in another way. They say, "Yes, I believe I ought to follow Jesus: but we live in such a complex and different age. How am I to be sure it still applies? I feel I am losing my grip. And I feel so alone in the stand that I am taking! I need help."

Every personal decision is also a decision about history. For the relativist, the most significant day in history is today. Yesterday is unimportant. Modern depth psychology, however, is pushing him back at least to his birthday. But if one would start dating checks by the date of his birth he would be in real trouble with the bank to say nothing about the merchant.

Flag-waving superpatriots in any country point to the birth of the nation. Nationalism is the single criterion. Other nations, though, may ask by what right the birth of one nation is more significant than that of another.

Academically we engage in another kind of sophistication. We divide history into ancient, medieval, and modern periods. With the help of radical evolutionism we give the impression or insist in an outright fashion as C. S. Lewis, Cambridge's converted atheist, testified he did before conversion: men were fools until about 100 years ago when what some have called the "myth of progress" began to fascinate man. We tend to attach derision and contempt to the "ancient" and the "medieval" and worship the "modern" even though we have outdone all ages in our lack of ability to get along with one another and our tremendous capacity for obliterating each other.

Modern man proudly resents any other focal point in history more crucial than the "now." Yet the amazing fact stands that ten times every day in the course of his work he looks at his calendar to relate himself to the "year of our Lord." Every important document in his life is worthless without that bit of — shall we not call it worship? Without it his life is out of relationship with all others. Theologian or not he has made a profound theological affirmation every time he dates a document! Oscar Cullmann, biblical theologian of the University of Basel and the Sorbonne, insists that our calendar has its roots in the biblical idea of time — that the coming of Christ stands at midpoint in human experience from which men are to view the totality of the future and the past.[2] Nothing in the future or the past has significant meaning apart from the incarnation, the atonement, and the resurrection!

It is a striking fact that this basic biblical orientation has fixed itself on our life so that radically empirical scientists engage in this unconscious but none the less real adoration of something in the past.

With Constantine the state, after only three centuries, fell at the feet of Jesus. Within about 200 years more the calendar, the most impervious, that most impenetrable of our institutions, was conquered by the humble Galilean! Men began to mark off time by His coming. What is probably just as startling is that at the very time when Christianity was heavily under fire by rationalists and atheists, the eighteenth-century men first began to reckon time before Christ in reverse. Thus the triumph of the gospel over the calendar was complete!

Never before, according to Cullmann, has it happened that men use one point in history and work *backward* as well as forward from that point. It is true that others take some point and work only forward. The Jews work forward from creation. The Romans worked forward from the foundation of Rome. In the third century, Emperor Diocletian, one of Christianity's most systematic persecutors, started the reckoning of time from his rule — *anni Diocletianni* which the Christians significantly called *anni martyrum*.[3] In 1792 during the French Revolution there was another attempt to pull the calendar back to zero and start again. But that failed, too. Presently there are no threats, including Sputnik.

Is it not a striking contradiction that proud self-sufficient modern man permits the past to dictate to him both in the matter of focal point for the reckoning of years and weeks? Months and years are dictated by nature but weeks and ages are dictated by history through the Bible. The calendar is the worship center that finds its way even into the home of the atheist and compels him to align part of his life to it.

Now Cullmann insists that this dating of years in reverse before Christ reflects a basic New Testament teaching that something happened with the coming of Christ which necessitates looking back over the whole of prior history again. Something happened that stands in a retroactive cause-and-effect relation to the years before Christ as it has stood in a prospective cause-and-effect relation to all that has followed.

The Lord Jesus Christ portrayed such stature that the four Gospel writers begin their story in one way or another according to the pattern of Genesis. The Gospel of John, Hebrews, and certain writings of Paul see Jesus, who was born in the reign of Herod, at work at the Creation. The whole New Testament sees Him at work at the end. He is sovereign over all time, regnant over all history. His reign extends from the cross back to creation and forward even as our calendar reflects. It is from this fundamental time perspective that this entire series of presentations is given. It is also the reason why this message is early in the series.

We must turn now directly to the Gospels and the Acts and see what it was that put the new calendar on the wall.

It was first of all a startling surprise from beginning to end. At every point it was so out of order *yet so compelling.* The wise men set Jerusalem in an uproar when they asked for the newborn king in the expected place, the palace, and then proceeded to find Him in a house in lowly Bethlehem. He was not clothed with purple in a gold-ornamented crib in a palace. The shepherds found Him homeless in a manger in a stable clothed in birthbands with commoners as attendants. He was not a mature deliverer bursting forth from the heavens but a determined young man going to the Jordan to join a young ascetic, John the Baptist, who

23

spoke to both temple and state and soon had his name on the list of undesirables. Jesus takes up the same challenging message loaded with chain-reaction power and proclaims that the kingdom of God is at hand. But to the amazement of all He gathers round Him not an army, which anything that called itself a kingdom surely ought to have, but a group of simple stalwart fishermen with the collaborating tax-collector, Levi, thrown in.

He declares war by sending the Twelve out to tell quickly that the long expected triumph of God is in process; when they return He congratulates them on their success for He has seen Satan cast from heaven. He prepares His men for the final phase of this initial yet definitive triumph by telling what to them was crushing news as to how the triumph would be achieved — death. They would have none of it! The old power-technique still had them in its grip — so much so that, as the record has it, they were still looking for a kingdom of force and arms after the resurrection (Acts 1:6)! They argued with Jesus; but when the final choice came they could only say, "Lord, to whom shall we go?" So unexpectedly surprising yet so imperiously compelling — this commander of a self-styled army of simple spokesmen, teachers, and healers. *This was the kingdom! This was war!* And the enemy — the devil, not men — was being crushed as the Commander Jesus fell mortally wounded at the head of His scattered army.

Another feature of the coming of Christ, this focal point of history, was its inclusiveness. Consider the way in which He personally identified Himself with the past of the chosen people — their destiny, their institutions, and their worship. No word of Jesus better explains His intense reverence for the past than the words, "Think not that I have come to abolish the law and the prophets . . . but to fulfil them. For truly, I say to you . . . not a dot will pass from the law until all is accomplished" (Mt. 5:17, 18). "Not to abolish . . . but to fulfil them." Jesus was no radical empiricist who insisted that "knowledge begins with me." What we have in Jesus is one who brings His own gifts to the totality of His past to live significantly in the present for the future. This is the biblically holistic view of man: man is intimately and inextricably involved in the totality of history.

In Nazareth, His hometown, He lays down the platform for His ministry quoting from Isaiah 61:1, 2 (Luke 4:18, 19):

> The Spirit of the Lord is upon me, because he
>   has anointed me to preach good news
>   to the poor.
> He has sent me to proclaim release
>   to the captives
>   and recovering of sight to the blind, to set at
>   liberty those who are oppressed, to proclaim
>   the acceptable year of the Lord.

We know that the Book of Isaiah, in speaking to help an exiled people (its purpose regardless of views on authorship and composition) drew heavily on the early narratives of the great deliverance from Egypt. Thus Jesus identifies Himself with the central concern of the law and prophets — deliverance or salvation of the people. His very name Jesus is the Greek for "Joshua" which means "deliverance" or liberation.

In portraying a father who gives his only son as indicated by John 3:16 and the parable about sending the son in Matthew 21 the New Testament answers the question of Isaiah's preparatory parable (5:4) where God asks searchingly, "What more was there to do for my vineyard?" In these we recall the aching father-heart of Abraham as he prepares to offer his son (Gen. 22) — the emphasis is clear —"His only son."

Like a Moses, Jesus takes His followers up into the mountain and gives the new law, the New Commandment. On the Mountain of Transfiguration a vision identifies Jesus with the law and the prophets when He appears with Moses and Elijah. The voice from heaven says for the benefit of Peter, James, and John, "This is my beloved Son; listen to him." Combined here is the kingly "My Son" motif of Psalm 2 and 2 Samuel 7:14 with the prophecy of the Second Moses (Deut. 18:15); when He comes the people are to hear Him.

The name Jesus used most in referring to Himself is "Son of man" which takes us back to Daniel, Ezekiel, and Psalm 8: "What is man, that thou art mindful of him? and the son of man, that thou visitest him?" Surely in Jesus, God was making a startling visitation of man. But probably as significant as either of these, "Son of man" means "son of Adam"; for *Adam* is one of the Hebrew words for man. Adam by his sin lost the image of God for the race; as promised, his seed, the son of man, second Adam, "came to seek and to save the lost" (Lk. 19:10).

We may select yet one more of a host of other instances where Jesus identifies Himself with the past. It is the instance where, while Jesus is giving announcements of His coming suffering, the disciples are arguing about chief places in the administration of the kingdom. Jesus reaches back into Isaiah and Exodus for the Servant motif as He says, "For the Son of man also came not to be served but to serve, and to give his life as a ransom for many" (Mk. 10:45). With the word "also" Jesus puts Himself into that royal line of servants, the prophets, and Moses who endured intense suffering as servants of the Word.

Yet Jesus was not a blotter that absorbed indifferently the past. To the past He brought His own gifts from God and left the past transfigured and transformed at every point! This

27

Man who transformed the calendar was not only inclusive in His attitude toward the past, He was normative — He showed a reverent criticism of the past. This criticism was *not* based on a newly injected principle. It was based rather on a living process of critical selection of the vital and living elements of the past — the work of the true prophet of God in the Old Testament. Thus He gave us a time orientation which we have hanging on our kitchen wall in the form of the calendar.

For many there remains one problem in all of this, particularly for those who are heavily involved in academic work. They rightly insist that written documents can get very distorted over such a long period of time. At this point archaeology has come to be of tremendous assistance. It is impossible to look at the Bible as men once did. There used to be essentially two points of view. Since one could not find the counterpart in other literature, some concluded the Bible obviously must be false. Others concluded it must be so great that it was surely dictated directly by God in its entirety. Those who say it is fiction are confronted with the name of Hezekiah in the annals of Sennacherib, the Assyrian king whose campaigns brought him to Palestine. These documents have been dug up from the dust heaps. The stones cry out to confirm that point. Or consider that the Nuzi and Mari tablets have legal customs from the second millennium

BC which are precisely the type recorded in the Bible for the time of Abraham. Of course the name of Abraham is not mentioned there, and one would hardly expect to find the name of Abraham because that is much too early a stage in the life of a people to find corresponding contemporary documents. It is, however, impossible to say with a former generation of Old Testament scholarship that the documents about Abraham were all composed in the time of David in order to explain the greatness of the glory of Israel and that the documents reflect essentially the type of life at the time of David. Consider also the time of the Babylonian captivity and Jehoiachin's ration tablets; this Israelite king who was taken into captivity and the information about the rations that were given him are also indicated in documents discovered in Mesopotamia. The Merneptah Stele, a victory record of an Egyptian king — actually mentions the name of the Israelites for thirteenth-century BC Palestine! Thus we may go on.

Now it must be clearly faced; archaeology does not solve all problems; it even turns up some problems. However, it is no longer possible to be radically skeptical about the essential historicity of the materials in the Old Testament. The problem of historicity of the Bible can no longer stand in the way of its serious claim for a reorientation of history in general as well as man's own personal history.

Once the history is written down the question may arise as to how one can be sure that in the long span of time through which this document was copied and recopied it has not been substantially altered. For what we have said about the biblical view of time is dependent upon the essential authenticity of the Bible.

Ask a student in American history how he knows that the Constitution as he finds it in the back of a history book is the one which the founding fathers actually wrote. Almost every history student will suggest going to Washington and looking at the original. One can see the original; one can take his books and place them side by side with it and see that they correspond. No one would be so bold in view of that evidence to say that change has taken place. Now, in the case of the Bible one is not quite in that situation because the documents as they were written down by the man who first penned them are no longer available. Only copies are available, but that is not to say that one need be skeptical. Great significance is to be attached to the recent discovery of the Dead Sea Scrolls as they bear upon our understanding of the essential dependability of the scribal transmission of the Bible. One may lay the complete Isaiah of 100-150 BC side by side with the present document. Supposing, in the case of the Constitution, that for a long time no copy of the Constitution was available earlier than

1875. Suddenly by the discovery of another copy from a period 1800 to 1820, there would be a jump of fifty years all at once. That would mean much if earlier materials were not available. Now in the case of the Dead Sea copy of Isaiah a jump of 1,000 years was made. The earliest manuscript before 1947 dated from around AD 900! Because it is true that there is comparatively minor change in that thousand years from the earliest material available (AD 900) to 100 BC, one is justified in assuming that surely there could not have been extensive change in the period from 100 BC back to the time of the writing of the book.

Thus archaeology is of great help. And more is to be expected. Professor W. F. Albright, world-famed orientalist and biblical archaeologist, says that only 5 percent of the archaeological resources of Palestine has been touched today. If the trend in present discovery is an indication of what may yet be expected there will be much more illustration and confirmation of the Scriptures though certainly not without an occasional problem.

All this underscores the authority with which the Bible insists that each one's name is written in this book when it says, "For God so loved the world, that he gave his only begotten Son, that whosoever believeth in him should not perish." Man's basic decision is somehow related to the Christ at the focal point of history, not to forty years ago when the Russian Revolution took place, not primarily to July 4, 1776, not to the date of a man's birth, or even to this day. Our decision is oriented, if we would be fighting in the right war, to Him who called the disciples and invited them to a massive warfare of teaching, healing, proclamation, suffering, death, and glory.

3 The Outfit
That Moves Forward as a Man
(Participation
in the Covenanted
Life in Christ)

No judgment upon modern man is greater than that he must find his deepest fulfillment in a fellowship of destruction. Even Mennonites seldom feel community as deeply as when others are caught in the web of war, and they are called upon for titanic relief efforts which weld them together with their fellows in need around the world. But alas! When the crisis is over and everybody goes back home it is everybody for himself with renewed vigor.

If for the moment we strip communism of its distinctively economic features, we may say that there are many communisms — many programs in the world that promise man unity, but which, in reality, only drive the wedges between man and man deeper. We may draw a line around Americans, around Russians, around Britishers and thus tighten the bonds; but when it is at the expense of excluding another nationality, the feeling of superiority over other nations tends to break out in our personal relations and we are more lonely than ever. We express our various national lonelinesses by erecting higher barriers and creating better weapons.

Strangely enough these fragmentizing systems of organization have infected the church, too, and we have denominationalism. But when the church sounds off on its denominational trumpet the inspiration is not from above or out of the Scriptures. For the basic thrust in the Bible is cohesion — not fragmentation.

Nowhere is this more evident than on the title pages of the two parts of our Bible, which but for a quirk of translation would be known among us as the Old Covenant and the New Covenant, for that is surely the original.

The word "covenant" has arisen out of a wealth of candidate words: witness, message, word, call, gospel, way, law, promise, prophecy, writings, scriptures — to mention a few that cut across both testaments. But covenant has risen to the top.[1] This is surely most interesting! The name for the two parts of the Bible comes from the continuing fundamental concept of interrelationship of person and person and God.

Further one may note that the Christian name for the Bible as covenant stands in sharp contrast to the Hebrew name for the Jewish Bible, the Old Testament — *Torah, Nebiim,* and *Kethubim*, which means Torah, Prophets, and Writings. "The Torah," meaning law or teaching, a pedagogical term, is also used to refer to the whole Old Testament. It refers, of course, to the fundamental revelation of God, Israel's teacher. But the Bible does not reflect a class-room situation in which God is in front cramming information down the throats of mankind!

In the course of time, then, covenant, the concern of a peaceful relationship between persons and persons and God by virtue of its titular position came to be regarded as the essence in all of life and existence that really matters. The biblical ontology involves persons in history, not nature or idea.

For our understanding of covenant we must see how indispensable some basis of interrelation among families in patriarchal or nomadic society really was. There was no larger structure of civil or national organization as in the Mesopotamian or Nile valleys. In Genesis we note settlements made between Isaac and his neighbors. A covenant is made that finally pacifies a turbulent relationship between Jacob and Laban, his father-in-law. In these purely human relations the peace of the community was built upon a covenant. This involved responsibility in the case of both parties!

George Ernest Wright[2] has pointed out that almost synonymous with "covenant" is the term "peace," which refers to an equitable harmonious relation with other persons and with God. Isaiah 54:10 has it thus: "For the mountains may depart and the hills be removed, but my steadfast love shall not depart from you, and my covenant of peace shall not be removed, says the Lord, who has compassion on you."

Particularly instructive is the context here. For intimately associated with covenant are such words as mercy, peace, and steadfast love. The latter term, "steadfast love" or "lovingkindness," as earlier versions have it, is really telescoping into two words the meaning of *chesed*, a Hebrew term that needs almost a sentence to express its meaning. It is the "responsible behavior which covenant relationship or blood relationship expects or assumes." Naomi, for example, commends Ruth and Orpah for such steadfast love for her as well as their husbands, Naomi's dead sons.

This language of the interrelationship of persons in their social relationship is the same language that is used in their relationship with God. It is supremely significant that Israelite language about God depicts Him almost solely in categories of personality and society and not nature as was so common among their pagan neighbors. You recall the portrayal of Ramses II, the Pharaoh of the Exodus, placing the body of his lifeless son upon the knees of the huge god Thoth, who had the body of a man but the head of a bird. What an unutterable chasm when something in nature rather than God the person is regarded as ultimate fulfillment! For the Israelite, then, as a person in community, there is an encounter with God as a person with whom he entered into relationships based on love and righteousness.

Often when we think of covenant we think of law and of good works which is very understandable! Perhaps the most solemn and high moment in all the Old Testament is the moment when, after the deliverance experience at the sea and the reception of the law Israel affirms thrice, "All that the Lord has spoken we will do" (Ex. 19:8; 24:3, 7). Moses erects an altar and twelve pillars to represent God and the twelve tribes. The covenant is sealed by sprinkling the blood of sacrifice on altar and pillars.[3]

The Lord was Israel's king and covenanted with Israel His subjects whom He offered the status of being His own people after the gracious acts of deliverance from Egypt. The conditions placed upon Israel were the worship of the Lord only and obedience to the fundamental laws of life in the Ten Commandments. When Israel obeys she will prosper; when she rebels she will be troubled.

But Israel was aware of another covenant more basic even than the Sinai Covenant about which we have been talking. In the fifteenth chapter of Genesis we note the record of another covenant (and this is clearly in the earlier strata of material). Abraham prepares the setting for the covenant ceremony. The animals are cut in two and placed on opposing sides symbolic of what should happen to Abraham if he does not obey God who has initiated the covenant. But at the critical moment a torch passes between the pieces symbolizing that the God who has commanded His servant Abraham actually takes upon Himself the obligations and makes Himself the servant of Abraham![4] Here there is no obligation whatsoever on Abraham. The covenant is unconditional! This is the basis for the inevitable optimism with regard to the long-range future of the people of God on the part of the prophets. Not even an Amos thundering doom could get to the end of his writings without a promise of recovery. In the midst of relapse after relapse after relapse of faith the Hound of Heaven still pursues and woos His people. The covenant of law and justice even in the Old Testament is set squarely in the context of grace!

If this is true of the Old Testament it is infinitely more true of the New Testament. The Great Commandment and the Sermon on the Mount portray the high demand placed on those who respond to the call of Christ. Here is the equivalent of the covenant of human obligation or law. That the term covenant is not used is quite beside the point when one considers how

Jesus' work paralleled that of Moses, not the least of which is the appointment or call of the Twelve and the seventy. But the corresponding event to the Genesis 15 account is the one place where the first three Gospels use the word covenant. It is at the institution of the Lord's Supper, "This is my blood of the covenant, which is poured out for many for the forgiveness of sins" (Mt. 26:28). This is unconditional; Christ nailed Himself to the human race on His cross till the last who wants it may accept. He demands, but He also descends to the lowest level of human need to walk upward with those who respond. Grace and law, love and responsibility are inseparable in God and in man.

In His disciples God is reaching out the hand of help we have seen in Christ. This is because of the intimate relationship the Christian bears to Christ. The Apostle Paul speaks of this relationship as the body (the disciples as the body of Christ) and ultimately of Christ comprehending all things in Himself. This means, then, that there can be no radical individualism other than the kind in which a man rips himself out of the grasp of God by a deliberate choice of utter independence from God, which is hell. It further means that in the Christian perspective each person is necessary to every other person. In the church every person is indispensable to every other person; there are no VIPs. I would further insist that this is important in the still unconverted humanity outside the church as well. For in the "inasmuch" of Jesus we understand that we actually meet our Lord in the person of the needy one — yes, even our enemy. God has bound us together into families, communities, and entire peoples that we may minister to one another. God Himself who created all this is so much involved in it that He embraced the whole with His outstretched arms on the cross and prayed, "Father, forgive them!" — ministering to all who will receive Him. "For God so loved the world!"

Everyone in a sense carries the world on his heart by virtue of the primary and secondary group relationships which he knows. If one lives in deliberate and prayer-sustained obedience to Jesus Christ, the totality of these immediate relationships will be bathed in the binding love of Christ. Like a stone cast upon water, the ripples must reach the most distant shore of existence. But there is no consciousness of the person being the cause of this; it is rather because he has yielded himself to One who merits every ounce of his devotion.

I am wondering whether the team on the athletic field may not know infinitely more about this close-knittedness of life than we do in the church. To win they must have respected leadership to which they can devote themselves unconditionally. This leadership teaches them infinite patience and understanding of one another and a rigor and toughness with self so that the mind of the coach by way of such devotion and discipline becomes the mind of the group. When the squad gets out on the field, you have eleven duplicates of the coach, who, operating as a team, move as a man. Yes, once in a while they will even pull off something the coach has not suggested but which a critical situation automatically calls out of the totality of their training. And we recall the words of the Master, "Greater works than these will he do." The amazing phenomenon — the coach who has lost himself in his players and the players who have lost themselves in the other players, the coach, and their alma mater's glory!

Dare we, I ask you, dare we give anything less to the Master of men, the Lord of the church? Dare we bristle up at every little personal inconvenience that others cause us — the equivalent incidentally of turning and making a touchdown for the opposing team? We forget that when we blow up at our roommate or life mate, we set back the forces of peace in the world. Our team, the church, is much too small to tolerate that!

4   Caught in the Deadly Cross Fire
(The   Kingdom
Among the Kingdoms)

The foundations of man's responsibility to others upon which the institutions of society rest reach back to the first page of the Bible and deep into the bedrock scriptural doctrine of creation. It all begins when God wills society. Both accounts of creation in Genesis give a very clear stratification between animal and human realms with man commanded to subdue the natural world. Both accounts put man and woman on the same plane. There is no basic stratification between man and woman. Furthermore, the pattern as indicated in Genesis is one of order in which, in the animate creation, the seed of reproduction is planted in each type of life with the command to reproduce: "Be fruitful and multiply!" To summarize, the command to man in relation to nature involves subduing or authority; the command in relation to persons is unity, equality, and creativity (but not destruction!).

The cataclysm that marks the Fall in Genesis three is a fundamental disruption of the order of creation. Man in his disobedience becomes mastered by nature at the suggestion of the serpent which represents the order of nature over which man was to reign. Nature (the serpent, later in the Scriptures, is called the devil) comes between man and God to fracture the fellowship of the order of creation. When God seeks the reason, man begins to make excuses by pointing the finger — "the woman!" Thus is fractured the unity of the sexes which according to the Bible has also left its scar on the equality and the creative aspects of the relation between man and woman. In the order of creation society is left in tender embrace. In the disorder of the Fall we have entered into finger-pointing — the era of fundamental irresponsibility — "the woman," "the serpent." Each proudly draws a false cloak of innocence around self and withdraws from the other.

From there the descending escalator carries man quickly from denial of responsibility for personal action to denial of responsibility for the brother as Cain answers God, "Am I my brother's keeper?" Man, who in one generation is pushed to arm's length, in the next is murdered. Five generations later Lamech celebrates the discovery of iron in terms of a boast of the multiple vengeance he has exacted. This is succeeded by unspeakable lust and finally the destruction of the Deluge.

Mankind is at the bottom of sin's descending escalator when God calls out Abraham to begin again. What we see at first seems to be a form of irresponsible separatism and favoritism: "Go from your country and your kindred and your father's house" (Gen. 12:1). But the positive side of the call indicates a broader purpose: "In you all the families of the earth shall be blessed" (Gen. 12:3, RSV, margin). Along with God's favor and commanded separatism is a promise that involves an obligation of universal dimensions. In the lifetime of Abraham himself there is already a distinct impact. While it is true that he is portrayed as a warrior, he is also portrayed as intercessor for his nephew to whom he allowed without strife the very choice of Canaan's lands. This magnanimity characterizes peaceful Isaac, the repentant Jacob, but above all divinely competent Joseph, who is instrumental in saving a great foreign nation from the ravages of famine while he insures the perpetuation of the chosen people.

Now archaeology has shown us that at the time when the Bible places Jacob's going down into Egypt, the Hyksos (sometimes called the Shepherd Kings) were probably in power in Egypt. It would be expected that they, being of

Semitic stock like Jacob, would understand the Hebrews. However, when they were driven out by a resurgence of native Egyptian rulers, this people Israel presented a serious national threat. So they began a series of ever intensified measures to oppress Israel.

Moses, surely by all odds the founder of the nation, was called out of the wilderness to announce to the oppressed people the day of deliverance. With nothing more than a shepherd's staff as a scepter of authority he called on the world's leading monarch to stop the oppression and turn his slaves loose. Instead the oppression was intensified! A horrible series of disasters came upon the land until it was clear to the monarch that he had met his equal. He let them go only to vacillate again. He dared God's wind but the reversing wind on the sea did not wait for Pharaoh's chariots.

Out of that experience Israel, a slave nation without a weapon except obedience, learned to call her Lord and ours a God of war (Ex. 15:3). Israel's sense of destiny was renewed. God tells them through Moses — and this is the real climax preparing the people for the instruction with the Ten Commandments in the wilderness — that they are to be a *kingdom* of priests, a holy *nation* (Ex. 19:5). Here in the earliest material in the Pentateuch, Israel is indicated as a highly privileged yet heavily obligated people. They are God's own possession, for all the earth is God's. But with such unequaled privilege she is involved in a heavier responsibility than any other of God's peoples. She is to be the mediator between the peoples and God.

The dual role of Abraham the father of Israel is repeated and developed in the nation. They are to be separated, holy; but they are to be separated so that they can be instrumental in ministering and mediating! Separation, yet identification. Apart, yet deeply involved. That is the divine command, the extremely difficult role of the people of God.

The pattern is further confirmed for Israel by the laws. The sense of responsibility for the foreigner is found in Israel's first law code called the Covenant Code. The Israelite is not to impose or permit labor on the Sabbath as regards the stranger in his gates (Ex. 20:10). The sojourner in Israel is protected by law from the oppression of the Israelite (Ex. 22:21; 23:9). Furthermore, from the earliest source in the Pentateuch it is clear that there is but one law for native and stranger (Ex. 12:49; Lev. 24:22; Num. 15:15f., 29). Of course, we should not forget the "mixed multitude" that went out of Egypt with Israel (Ex. 12:38) who, while they were undoubtedly difficult for Israel to assimilate and surely explain some of the murmuring and disobedience, were nonetheless never disowned of their part with Israel.

All this expression of responsibility is deeply interwoven with a sharp command of separation from the Canaanites whose current religious practices (involving even ceremonial prostitution) are to be utterly abhorred (Ex. 23:24, 32). They actually understood God as commanding extermination of those with such corrupt practices (Ex. 23:31).

However, we are not to assume from this that there is a universal aversion in the Old Testament for other people as such. At her best Israel realizes that she has a mission to others. She dare not cut herself off. But her mission is one of faith, and being such she must have nothing whatsoever to do with the faith or the gods of the neighbors. Such a position demanded maturity. Alas! Israel was always trying to settle for something less.

One way of avoiding creative-separatism was to put the accent on understanding others even to a point that was naked compromise. They would have a golden calf during the feast of the Lord (Ex. 32:4-6). They would be internationally minded and erect pagan shrines for the foreign wives of the kings (2 Kings 11:1-8).

Another way of getting around the appointed yet difficult position was to "ride" the "separate people" doctrine so hard they had little time to consider why they were to be separate! They developed a "race" doctrine that called forth severe protests in the books of Ruth and Jonah.

While the Book of Ruth clearly fills the gap in the genealogy down to David and further illustrates the unsettled conditions in the time of the Judges (which book it follows in the Old Testament), it keeps needling the segregationists by referring repeatedly to Ruth, the Moabitess, the descendant from incest (Gen. 19:30-38). But Ruth proved to have the heart of a true Israelite and she is honored with a place in the royal family tree despite her own questionable family tree.

Or consider the Book of Jonah, that supreme missionary document of the Old Testament. Called of God to preach to non-Jews at Nineveh, Jonah runs off in the opposite direction. Consider the tremendous lengths to which God had to go to get him to the place where He wanted him. His evangelistic campaign was a tremendous success but Jonah was still displeased that God was showing favor to foreigners. God was concerned over man, woman, and child, and even cattle in "pagan Nineveh." All of us know attitudes toward certain groups which would leave us almost disappointed if God chose to save them!

We must retrace our steps now and note briefly the organizational structure through which Israel and the church gave expression to their way of thinking about their larger social relationships and obligations.

The responsive family unit built around a believing father is twice emphasized in Genesis (Noah and Abraham) as the *sine qua non,* the true foundation without which a responsible society cannot arise.

Built directly upon this was the community of families as indicated in Exodus and especially Numbers. The pattern of the camp is one in which the tabernacle is at the center with three Levitical families who serve the tabernacle at its sides and back and the sons of Aaron at the front, Moses and Aaron being at the door. At the outside of this central complex are the twelve tribes distributed according to number (for the statistics in Numbers are of fighting men) with the heaviest concentration to the east and the lightest to the west. The twelve tribes were also responsible to provide for the materials for sacrifices. Noteworthy up to this point are several things: (1) the universal, interlocking, and interdependent responsibility of all for the whole; (2) the mediating function of the Levites; and, (3) the direct access of all, through the Levites, to the tabernacle.

Striking in all this is the tabernacle with its two rooms — the holy place and the holy of holies. The holy of holies contains the ark and the mercy seat from between whose cherubim the voice (but not the person) of God speaks! The holy of holies is then, in reality, a throne room![1] This is a people with an empty throne, an invisible King! (Cf. Ex. 15:18). Moses the

49

mighty leader of Israel is but His servant (Ex. 14:31).

If Israel is to be a kingdom of priests, a holy nation in relation to the other nations of the world, then we must assume that this is the pattern for her relation to the nations around the empty throne of the living God. Israel becomes, like the Levites, mediating; the non-Israelite nations of the world as the twelve tribes. The prophecy of Isaiah, much later, does in fact portray all nations coming up to the mountain of the Lord (Is. 2:2-4).

Israel was to be ruled by the unseen King of the heavens and the earth; Israel was not to put a human being on that empty throne and call him God as many nations were doing. This helps us understand the seriousness of the situation when the people at a later time clamored for a king. They were to have servants or judges as they were called. When the people did finally get their wish and set up a human throne in the temple-complex with the divine throne, it was really quite a different kind of monarchy. The limitations on it as compared with other contemporary absolutisms is manifest in Nathan's power as God's prophet to come to the king and condemn him for stealing another man's wife as well as plotting the man's death in the process!

Alongside the development of the monarchy was the growth of the prophetic office — the role of the man who spoke for the one and only authority in heaven and earth who has ultimate power. The prophet spoke to the nation, symbolized by the ruler, concerning the divine directives. There was a clear weddedness of church and state, with secular authority subservient to religious authority. When the earthly throne was shaken the prophet would point to the heavenly throne which remained unshaken (Is. 6). Thus the office of king in Israel was really incidental — a concession, God's second best for Israel; the prophetic office, the office of the word, remained the primary line through which God was working. Thus, it is to be expected that John the Baptist and Jesus take their place in this primary task in the true Israel — speaking for rather than trying to rule in the place of the King of heaven and earth.

Furthermore we should point out that human discipline and warfare are likewise secondary, not primary! When we compare Israel's laws with those of the other nations we encounter two surprises: the similarity between the case laws in Exodus 21-23 and other ancient law codes on the one hand; and the uniqueness of the Ten Commandments on the other hand. In range of coverage and even form the latter are not duplicated anywhere in antiquity. In Exodus the Ten Commandments appear to be the foundation on which the details of the case laws are constructed. But impressive is the fact that nowhere in the Ten Commandments is there a direct mandate for human discipline! Certain things will come to those who obey or disobey but this comes from God. One of the earliest cases of discipline is the situation of the earth swallowing up the rebels Korah, Dathan, and Abiram (Num. 16:32, but compare Ex. 32:25-29). The discipline was divinely executed.

Turning to warfare, the great defeat of Egypt which reverberates all through the Bible was a weaponless victory! The Pharaoh against his better judgment dared God's wind and lost! Beyond this our best study of the phenomenon of war in the Old Testament reveals two types of warfare which roughly correspond to the two periods noted above — the period of Moses and the Judges on the one hand and the period of the monarchy on the other.[2] In the early period little is made of weapons and numbers, only faith in God's cause and strict obedience. This sometimes involved complete destruction of the foe in a kind of sacrifice. This does not appear to be a warfare based on foreign policy. During the monarchy, however, the army becomes a tool of the monarch. At Megiddo archaeologists have found the stables from the time of the monarchy, evidence of a standing army. But the prophets who stood up to the kings called for a policy of faith instead of frantic preparation in the case of Isaiah and submission rather than use of force in the case of Jeremiah. From these two prophets primarily the New Testament and its key personalities draw most heavily for inspiration. From the standpoint of the Old Testament, then, viewed from the high and normative points of the Exodus, Isaiah, Jeremiah, and even King David (the founder of the dynasty of Jesus Christ was unfit to build the temple because of bloody hands of war), is it any wonder that we move into a cloudless pacifist sky in the New Testament? The very name of New Testament (New Covenant) is drawn from the book of that "traitor" who suggested capitulation without resistance — Jeremiah!

In the New Testament as well as the Old Testament, political responsibility has an added dimension which makes it totally different from anything in other countries or other powers and renders it potentially in conflict with both. It was built around faith in the invisible, omnipotent, almighty, spiritual God who needed men but not their self-sufficient fleshly strength.

John the Baptist and Jesus both keynoted their ministries with "The kingdom of heaven is at hand" (Mt. 3:2; 4:17), a distinctly political cry; but then instead of saying, "Arm yourselves and train," they said, "Repent . . . believe . . . follow . . ." (Mk. 1:15-17). This was indeed a strange call to arms. But make no mistake; it was a call to arms!

This cry was raised at a time when it might have been mistaken for one of a number of attempts at armed revolt against the occupying Romans. Except for a few it lost its attractiveness to the Jewish leadership because it did not promise political liberty. It lost its threat to Rome because it was not an armed movement. But the common people took up the cry in a way that neither Rome nor Judaism could ignore and save face. So Jesus was crucified when He was caught between the fire of two temporal powers — Jerusalem and Rome.

But in the whole process Jesus went about His work in a way that was strangely reminiscent of one who had led the children of Israel through the first deliverance. They were convinced that here was the prophet God would raise up like Moses (Deut. 18:15). According to the Gospels He gathered twelve around Him (Mt. 10:1 f.). In the synagogue at Nazareth He read from Isaiah 61:1-3, a passage which drew its inspiration from Moses, "He has sent me to proclaim release to the captives . . . to set at liberty those who are oppressed. . . ." He did a whole series of signs (according to John) encountering hardening and unbelief as Moses had according to Exodus. He went up into a mountain and gave them the new commandments (Mt. 5:1; cf. Jn. 13:34). He appointed seventy to speed the work even as Moses had (Ex. 19). He referred to His body as the temple He was building and when He said, "It is finished" (Jn. 19:30), He was echoing Exodus 40:33, "So

Moses finished the work." Moses was ready to let himself be blotted out for the people (Ex. 32:32); and Jesus was.[3]

Peter felt the kingdom's hopes were disintegrating when the high priest's soldiers came after Jesus. He drew the sword. With Jesus' answer went the excuse of self-defense as He healed the ear. "Put up thy sword. . . ." The final answer for the disciples came after the resurrection in the form of the Great Commission. In Acts 1:6 the disciples asked: "Wilt thou at this time restore again the kingdom to Israel?" (KJV). The answer is clear; the times and seasons are up to God but they would receive power to witness. Jesus had said the kingdom is here. They were about to enter its full power at Pentecost when they would wield the weapon of witness all over the world before the consummation at the return of Christ.

Admittedly in the ministry of Jesus and the apostles there appears to be a certain blindness or obliviousness to political responsibility. But this is only on the surface. Taxes should be paid; those in authority are to be honored and supported in prayer. The latter was enjoined in nonbiblical writings during a persecution thought by some to be the one calling forth the Book of Revelation. Few of those in public service in the New Testament (the soldiers and centurions, Zacchaeus) are recorded as leaving it. But of course this argues from silence which is always precarious. Paul had no hesitation in claiming his rights as a Roman. Jesus also raised the question about rights.

Having said all this, however, one must not forget the sense of priority growing out of intense urgency that the first Christians had about the kingdom. We still live in this interim period between the two comings of Christ. Further, talents most needed by the state are frequently the ones the church most needs. A young person who has qualities that would make for superior performance in politics and who is also a dedicated Christian will have an extremely difficult decision to make. I firmly believe he can serve God in the service of the state but he will need to realize that in his person two kingdoms stand in conflict — the kingdom of force and the kingdom of persuasion. He can accomplish a signal triumph for Christ if he is true, but it will be at a high price.

In a limited sense each one plays this role. Some say we must have nothing to do with the state, an institution which is for the pagan world. Others say that if a pacifist is an officer of the state he cannot act according to a belief to which the state has not attained; he must act according to the state's belief.[4] Jesus' stance, however, is one of complete identification with man in love and complete judgment of man in love. Anything less does violence either to the doctrine of creation or the doctrine of redemption and ignores the cross by which we are permitted to enter at the profoundest level into an identification with man's aching need for God and God's bleeding heart for man.

5 The Kingdom's Tactical Supremacy
(Incarnation and Substitution vs. Idolatry and Irresponsibility)

Incarnation (God was in Christ) and substitution (Christ died for us) are words of first magnitude of importance in developing our way of thinking about the nature, mission, and work of Christ. We have not been accustomed, however, to apply them to our way of thinking about our own nature as Christians and our mission.

We have earlier pointed out that the covenant erases the distance between God and man. We have stressed the crucial power of the word-deed of love. It follows then that doctrine and ethics cannot be separated and that Christology and anthropology must be kept together for the mutual benefit of both.

We fear dishonoring Christ by bringing Him too close to man; we fear deifying man by bringing him too close to Christ. In the Bible we do not find such abnormal fear of mixing the two to the detriment of either. The very opposite fear is expressed! Fear is expressed lest denial is made of Jesus' coming in the flesh (1 Jn. 4:2); Paul constantly insists that the church is the body of Christ and chides the Corinthian Christians for failing to remember that their body is the very temple of the Holy Spirit (1 Cor. 6:19).

We must once more recapture that biblical sense of deep interrelationship between God and man in Jesus the Christ. If we can do that we are bound to recover unsuspected areas of personal responsibility. Much more than that, we will discover unsuspected resources to meet those responsibilities. This is a thrilling discovery! Finally we will uncover unsuspected areas of idolatry and irresponsibility. This may be shocking.

Nothing has been quite as devastating to our sense of deep involvement in the incarnation of Christ as the heresy of testamental Christianity.[1] Our common thought about the Bible sees the Old Testament on a low level though we are ready to grant a gradual rise in that level. With the Gospel of Matthew, however, we commonly shift in our thinking to a very high level. With this erroneous conception of the relation of the two testaments we have pushed Jesus above our level of life and have skimmed off His words from His person turning them into principles which are much easier to ignore than the life of one who lives on our own plane. Whether in the overemphasis on the deity of Christ or in the deification of principle (both done in such a way that permits us to excuse our sin) we arrive at a point far short of the "fullness of the stature of Christ." We have surely "come short of the glory of God."

The first page of the New Testament is a perfect illustration of how we are to think of Christ. In our ordinary reading we quickly skip over the monotonous genealogy to get to the Christmas story. How we dwell on the uniqueness of Christ! And I am not suggesting that we should forget the virgin birth! For me it has an integral place. But proportionwise look at the earthiness, the human side of Jesus! Seventeen verses of genealogy show His deep roots in humanity. The line is hardly a pure one: Abraham, the father of the faithful was also a liar and polygamist; David, the founder of the kingly line, an adulterer. The deep roots in the Old Testament are indicated by the first sentence, "The book of the genealogy. . . ." which is a takeoff on the literary structure of Genesis so that the whole gospel is to be understood as a second beginning closely connected with that very human first beginning. Finally, at the close of the chapter Matthew is reminded of Isaiah's Immanuel, the sign King Ahaz rejected. The name in that context is to be reassurance to

Ahaz who with Jerusalem is panic-stricken because of the coalition between the Northern Kingdom and Syria against Judah and Jerusalem (Is. 7:1). The name means "with us is God." What this should say to Ahaz is, "Remember you are in a coalition with God — the King of heaven and earth! Your hope and your deliverance is in a newly born child — Immanuel." Isaiah also points out the price of ignoring the sign in unbelief.

While "Immanuel" is used but twice in the Old Testament (Is. 7 and 8), it epitomizes the central thread of Old Testament promise which occurs again and again: "I will be with you." Psalm 46, from which Luther got "A Mighty Fortress Is Our God," has this refrain:

> The Lord of Hosts is *with us*,
> The God of Jacob is our refuge.

The psalmist associates this God who is present with His people with the "God of Jacob." Reading the experiences of Jacob in Genesis will recall that at Bethel (Gen. 28) the central promise in the ladder-dream experience was "I am with thee." It is also crucial in Moses' constant struggle from his acceptance of the commission to his working with the people. This whole rich experience of God and of His presence by His people as it is gathered up in the name Immanuel comes to a brilliant focus in the Son of God in the flesh. This experience in both testaments may be summed up in this: God is totally and aggressively accessible to man through Christ who is the living historical manifestation of the continuing immediate experience by Israel of His saving presence. Reality withholds nothing from a totally responsive man.

That man has the capacity for this is implicit in our doctrine of creation where man is created in the image of God and carries on where God leaves off in the naming process (Gen. 2:19).

There is a direct similarity between Moses and Jesus. God told Moses, "You shall be to him [Pharaoh] as God" (Ex. 4:16). This, I am convinced, extends to us as Paul (Gal. 2:20) said, "I am crucified with Christ: nevertheless I live; yet not I, but Christ liveth in me."

In addition to the incarnation of God in His people and in Christ there is yet a sin-neutralized incarnation of God in everyone. This is testified to in both testaments. In the judgment scene of Matthew (25:40, 45) to ignore the needy one whether a child of God or not is to leave God out in the cold. Jacob is reconciled to Esau (Gen. 33) after the night of wrestling followed by the testimony, "I have seen thy face," he says (33:10), "I have seen thy face as one seeth the face of God" (ARV).

In this universal indwelling of God in man, either as actively recognized or as neutralized by sin, we find the basis of loving God and neighbor as himself. When we destroy others we are destroying not only God, but also self since in God our own self cannot be separated from the self we destroy in others. The refusal to take the life of another is not a peripheral biblical concern championed by a few eccentrics. It is the inescapable essence of Christianity's most distinctive and foundational conviction — the incarnation.

The incarnation, mighty step of God to participate *in* our human life, is but the setting of the stage for the second phase of God's work which is *for* man. We live in a world of right and wrong that has its own built-in judgment. The race with which Christ identified Himself is one which has actively sinned judgment upon itself. Each man's sins catch him short in a way his conscience cannot deny in spite of any attempted proud protestations. God in Christ not only came to stand with us but has gone further and assumed the guilt which our consciences feel so heavily. "Why, one will hardly die for a righteous man — though perhaps for a good man one will dare even to die. But God shows his love for us in that while we were yet sinners Christ died for us" (Rom. 5:7, 8). God not only comes to us in the remote place of judgment and separation where sin has taken us; in Christ He also paves a way back. Here is the God of the second mile, for it means the toleration of sin (not committed, of course, but taken upon Himself); that which He has forever set

Himself against is taken into His own nature. "For our sake he made him to be sin who knew no sin, so that in him we might become the righteousness of God" (2 Cor. 5:21). With that man who accepts full responsibility for his shabby past with full face toward Christ — with that man Christ is not ashamed to walk through life or to stand before God in judgment.

Here is God's treatment of His enemies in Romans 5:10: "For if while we were enemies we were reconciled to God by the death of his Son, much more, now that we are reconciled, shall we be saved by his life." The immediate application is in the Sermon on the Mount, "But I say to you, Love your enemies and pray for those who persecute you, so that you may be sons of your Father who is in heaven" (Mt. 5: 44, 45). That this is to be our practice too is indicated in John 15:12: "This is my commandment, that you love one another as I have loved you. Greater love has no man than this, that a man lay down his life for his friends. You are my friends if you do what I command you." I am convinced that there is a basic evident continuity of both incarnation *and* substitution from Jesus to us. Here is a willingness to take or share in the consequences of the wrong act of another even if we have had no part whatsoever in the wrong act; this is in order to help restore integrity in and fellowship with the wrongdoer. The effectiveness of accepting or sharing those consequences can only be sure as we share the purity of Christ on the one hand and completely identify ourselves with the wrongdoer on the other.

The sacrifices of the Old Testament said this; the animal had no part in the cause of the evil. In the laying on of the hand of the sinner a forced identification (without the will of the animal) takes place. Now consider the powerful impact on the sinner when he had to look upon perfect specimens of God's good creation pouring out their blood time after time for the atonement of the sinner. The Old Testament does not uniformly portray animal sacrifices; it also envisions human sacrifice. Moses in his prayer of intercession at the sin of the golden calf says, "But now, if thou wilt forgive their sin — and if not, blot me . . . out" (Ex. 32:32). The Servant in Isaiah who is sometimes Israel but cannot be regarded only as Israel, of his own will bears the sin of many (Is. 53). The early church sees Jesus as this "Holy servant" who gave His life for the atonement of others. Finally Paul in Romans 12:1 pleads, "I appeal to you therefore, brethren, by the mercies of God, to present your bodies as a living sacrifice, holy and acceptable to God." The practical expression of this follows in this chapter in the relationship of the Christian to various categories of persons in the church and outside including antagonists or enemies of the Christian.

Now these two most crucial and fundamental doctrines stress several things. One of these is that conflict can only be effectively dealt with in a direct relationship between persons. It further depends on the aggressive initiative of persons in the establishment of such a relationship. The motive of that initiative is the tender concern for the total welfare of the other person — the love which is ready to pour out its very life for the other.

This is deeply rooted in the very structure of biblical thought — this ultimate concentration upon the cruciality of the personal and the personalization of the institution. We see this in the Gospel of John. You will recall that the Pharisees came to Jesus and asked Him about His authority in connection with His cleansing the temple, and He made this statement: "Destroy this temple, and in three days I will raise it up" (Jn. 2:19). But they missed the point. He was talking about His body; they were thinking about an earthly building. When we come to the end of John's Gospel, only John's Gospel has this word from the cross, "It is finished!" Usually, and to a certain extent correctly, it is seen to mean that God's provision for salvation is now complete. But there may be a connection between that phrase and the conception of His very body as the temple. Moses erected the tabernacle which was the meeting place between God and sinful humanity by way of Israel. So Jesus in the purity of His own flesh and in the constant outgoing of His own love, the expression of the love of the Father, turned His very body into the eternal temple. This temple makes possible the meeting of the enemy — the sinner, the man who is going in the opposite direction from God yet who got his very existence and his body from God — and the God who is constantly in search of him.

This brings us to the concern of our irresponsibility and idolatry. When we see no more in the temple or our churches than mere buildings, and if we have not that similar concern to carry about in our very body churches, meeting places between man and God, then our churches and our bodies become an idol. We use them to exalt self and perpetuate barriers. They become ends in themselves. Rather, our bodies, like the body of Christ, are to be a battleground where the trying conflicts of our time are staged. These conflicts are to be fought not at arm's length taking up the weapons of nature, but within our hearts, as we separate ourselves from the world in order that we may gather into our arms that same sinful world in reconciliation. That is what our bodies are to be. They are to be living replicas of the tabernacle and the temple. We should come to think more and more when we say church, not of brick and mortar, but of flesh and blood. For while flesh and blood express the depths of collapse of God's creation on one hand, in Christ they express also the signal victory of God's creation.

You and I, then, are to regard our lives as the meeting places, as the battlegrounds for these conflicts so that they do not spread out into the realm of the shedding of blood with human instruments of destruction. This helps us to understand what Paul meant when he said that we struggle not against flesh and blood, but against principalities, against powers, against the hosts of wickedness in heavenly places. Therefore, he suggests the suitable instrument to cope with the true nature of the enemy, the breastplate of righteousness. If we are contaminated, we are ineffective. The sword of the spirit which is the word of God, our feet shod with the preparation of the gospel of peace — both are the instruments of personality rather than the physical instruments of destruction, and they alone have the promise of victory.

6 Turning Battle Songs into Hymns of Peace
(The Celebration of the Lordship of Christ)

The New Testament church was in the business of demilitarizing Old Testament battle songs.

Every great cause must have in addition to its psychological, sociological, historical, and personal awarenesses a really penetrating poetic awareness. The people who set the music and the metaphors of a civilization, a nation, or a faith are bound to take captive the hearts of the people. If it is true, as someone has said, that a metaphor can penetrate a crack much too small for a definition, then a cause that seeks to win the world must have mastery of metaphors.

The New Testament was heir to some brilliantly and shockingly nationalistic poetry that had served effectively to bind the Jews into a firm militant unity. These the New Testament church under the lordship of Christ was converting into militant hymns of peace.

What could be more haughty and brutally nationalistic than the two best known Messianic Psalms, especially in some of their parts? Since these two Psalms (2 and 110) form the basis of this presentation and since we need to examine them carefully to appreciate their force, we quote them in full. Psalm 2 reads as follows:

Why do the nations conspire,
 and the peoples plot in vain?
The kings of the earth set themselves,
 and the rulers take counsel together,
 against the Lord and his anointed, saying,
"Let us burst their bonds asunder,
 and cast their cords from us."

He who sits in the heavens laughs;
 the Lord has them in derision.
Then he will speak to them in his wrath,
 and terrify them in his fury, saying,
"I have set my king
 on Zion, my holy hill."

I will tell of the decree of the Lord:
He said to me, "You are my son,
 today I have begotten you.
Ask of me, and I will make the nations your
  heritage,
 and the ends of the earth your possession.
You shall break them with a rod of iron,
 and dash them in pieces like a potter's vessel."

Now therefore, O kings, be wise;
 be warned, O rulers of the earth.
Serve the Lord with fear,

with trembling kiss his feet,
lest he be angry, and you perish in the way;
   for his wrath is quickly kindled.

Blessed are all who take refuge in him.

Note also how harsh and bloody Psalm 110
sounds to our ears:
The Lord says to my lord:
   "Sit at my right hand,
till I make your enemies
   your footstool."

The Lord sends forth from Zion
   your mighty scepter.
   Rule in the midst of your foes!
Your people will offer themselves freely
   on the day you lead your host
   upon the holy mountains.
From the womb of the morning
   like dew your youth will come to you.
The Lord has sworn
   and will not change his mind,
"You are a priest for ever
   after the order of Melchizedek."

The Lord is at your right hand;
   he will shatter kings on the day of his wrath.
He will execute judgment among the nations,
   filling them with corpses;
he will shatter chiefs
   over the wide earth.
He will drink from the brook by the way;
   therefore he will lift up his head.

To harness earthly power with divinity and

then link them both to the fiery emotion of poetry is to produce a composition that will quickly latch hold of the imagination and dedication of whole peoples and throw them headlong into brutal warfare and bloodshed.

One senses that these Psalms must have been ringing in the ears of the restless Jews as they were thinking of deliverance from those who had taken them a captive nation. Otherwise, how can you explain the fact that two of the dominant motifs of the New Testament appear to be traceable to these very Psalms? From the Second Psalm comes the motif, "Thou art my son." From the 110th Psalm is the motif, "the right hand." The New Testament writers appear to have deliberately ripped these metaphors out of their context of nationalism, earthly power, and brutality (blessed breach of all exegetic procedure!) and used them to compose a new hymn of imperialism, the imperialism of love and truth and righteousness and judgment.

In the first chapter of the Epistle to the Hebrews, these two motifs are brilliantly combined. Twice is the "my son" motif applied to Jesus and twice the "right hand" motif applied not to one who reigned on a throne but one who died on a cross. Furthermore, all this follows hard on one of the best sentences that sums up both testaments: "In many and various ways God spoke of old to our fathers by the prophets; but in these last days he has spoken to us by a Son.

. . ." There is essential continuity between the word of the prophet and the living Word. This still stands if Hebrews 13:8 means anything: "Jesus Christ is the same yesterday and today and for ever." The Scriptures say one thing and only one: self-sacrificing love is ever the only ultimate reality.

Let us consider then the strategic and constructive use that is made of these motifs in other parts of the New Testament. The "my son" expression is determinative in the first three Gospels and the Acts — material that has been regarded as the most untheological part of the New Testament! Turn, for example, to Luke 3:21: "Now when all the people were baptized, and when Jesus also had been baptized and was praying, the heaven was opened, and the Holy Spirit descended upon him in bodily form, as a dove, and a voice came from heaven, 'Thou art my beloved Son; with thee I am well pleased.' " [1] "The son," who piles up the corpses in the Old Testament, applied to our Lord Jesus Christ, is stripped of all military power in this expression of the voice from heaven saying, "Thou art my beloved Son; with thee I am well pleased." This is doubly significant when we consider what Jesus had just done. He had followed the multitude that emptied the temple courts of Jerusalem, going down to Jordan to hear "the Voice," as John the Baptist spoke of himself. Jesus identifies Himself with this austere group that cut itself off from any show of earthly power so pompously paraded by the ritual and riches of the power-hungry religious leaders of His day.

At another exceedingly crucial turning point in Jesus' life (Lk. 9:28-36), the words come again from heaven. He has just announced to the disciples after Peter's great confession, "Thou art the Christ, the son of the living God," that He will achieve His mission through suffering and death; but Peter, spokesman that he was for the group as we are told in Mark, "took him, and began to rebuke him." This brought from Jesus the sternest rebuke that any of His disciples ever got: "Get behind me, Satan! For you are not on the side of God, but of men." It also brought from Jesus the most heart-searching order for the soldiers of the cross: "If any man would come after me, let him deny himself and take up his cross and follow me." Crosses are for rebels, Peter must have thought, not for the faithful army. But the transfiguration follows in which Jesus appears with Moses, representing the Law, and with Elijah, the Prophets. Again a voice comes from heaven like the one at the baptism: "This is my Son, my Chosen," but this time it is followed with words, not of approval for Jesus but of command for the disciples, "Listen to him."

These words are jolting enough when we consider that heaven hereby confirms the way of the cross, but given in the presence of Moses these words are doubly startling, for the people were eagerly looking forward to the coming of a prophet according to the words of Moses in Deuteronomy 18:15: "The Lord your God will raise up for you a prophet like me from among . . . your brethren — him you shall heed."

The voice from heaven like the ancient prophecy said, "Listen to him." Any careful study of the life of Jesus will show a host of parallels to the life of Moses as we have pointed out before. The disciples become aware suddenly that they have in their midst one with the towering stature of a Moses, the creator under God of a community. This Jesus then becomes the creator of the new community, the new society. This hard command of the cross received the double confirmation of the Law and Heaven. His step to the throne of universal power, then, was not to be on the head of vanquished and slaughtered foes, but from a cross on which He Himself died. One cannot help feeling that what was desired in the way in which the Gospels were put together was that as those motifs appear at those particular places, the people are reminded to go back and to read the whole Psalm. Thus they might have before them the ancient picture of the Messiah on the one hand and Jesus, the heaven-approved Messiah, on the other. They were to see the incongruity of it and realize that Jesus' way is truly the way of the God of power.

That the resurrection at the end of the Gospels is the third and the final voice from heaven may be noted from Acts 13:32 where we read, "And we bring you the good news that what God promised to the fathers, this he has fulfilled to us their children by raising Jesus; as also it is written in the second psalm,

> You are my son,
> today I have begotten you."

Here is even specific documentation. He is urging them to go back and read the second psalm. They are to go back and read the second psalm in this context and get their doctrine of the Messiah straightened out. This is Luke's report of the preaching of Paul in Antioch of Pisidia to the Jews who were expecting the Messiah. Paul fearlessly rips this precious proof text out of the hands of materialistic and nationally minded Jews and writes it over the empty tomb of true Israel's monarch, the Lamb that was slain. They would have real difficulty at this point. For a prime text for His coming in power here is applied to His coming in humility and suffering.

What is true of Luke's writing is true also of Matthew and Mark. The amazing, startling, compelling, and overwhelming audacity of these Gospel writers was to take this precious text of the radical patriots and write it over the life of the humble carpenter of Nazareth whose only army was the fishermen and a tax collector. His only weapon was the word-deed of love, infinite patience and suffering, and the throne of the cross. What a strange combination, and yet, what a compelling combination! For twenty centuries men have tried to ignore, even stamp it out, only to have the Hound of Heaven hounding them; and they return, embrace it, and are saved.

"The right hand" is another motif symbolizing power in the Old Testament. In Israel's national anthem (Ex. 15), the song of Moses at the Red Sea, where it specifically says, "The Lord is a man of war," these words are mentioned three times (vv. 6, 12):

> Thy right hand, O Lord, glorious in power,
>   thy right hand, O Lord, shatters the enemy.
>
> Thou didst stretch out thy right hand,
>   the earth swallowed them.

Now in the other of our fiery Messianic Psalms (110), which has the superscription, "A Song of David," we note the following words:

> The Lord says to my lord:
>   "Sit at my right hand,
>   till I make your enemies your footstool."

"Right hand" turns up in the most unexpected places in the New Testament. For example, it is found in Peter's sermon at Pentecost. He says, "This Jesus God raised up, and of that we are all witnesses. Being therefore exalted at the right hand of God, and having received from the Father the promise of the Holy Spirit, he has poured out this which you see and hear" (Acts 2:32, 33). Here is no rod of iron lording it over the victim, but a cleansing spirit prodding burdened consciences into the blessed subjection of the redeemed.

This motif turns up again in Ephesians 1:19-22 in a context that piles up more words for power than perhaps any other in Scripture. Paul is praying for them that they may know "what is the immeasurable greatness of his power in us who believe, according to the working of his great might which he accomplished in Christ when he raised him from the dead and made him sit at his right hand in heavenly places, far above all rule and authority and power and dominion, and above every name that is named, not only in this age but also in that which is to come; and he has put all things under his feet and has made him the head over all things for the church." This weak organization that set itself to win the world by word and deed instead of by force and power is the very body of Him who is on the throne. This weak little circle of Christians is the deep concern and the mighty instrument of Him who is at the right hand of power.

When the writer of Hebrews makes his main point in 8:1, 2 he says, "Now the point in what we are saying is this: we have such a high priest, one who is seated at the right hand of the throne of the Majesty in heaven, a minister in the sanctuary and the true tent which is set up not by man but by the Lord." Here is mingled power and the mediatorial work of the priestly office. The manner of coming to both of those significant functions is the way of the cross. Furthermore, in pointing up the finality of the work of Christ, and its absolute unrepeat-ableness, Hebrews 10:11-13 says, "And every priest stands daily at his service, offering re-peatedly the same sacrifices, which can never take away sin. But when Christ had offered for all time a single sacrifice for sins, he sat down at the right hand of God, then to wait until his enemies should be made a stool for his feet." As the writer begins the final thrust of the document (Heb. 12:1, 2), he says, "Therefore, since we are surrounded by so great a cloud of witnesses, let us also lay aside every weight, and sin which clings so closely, and let us run with perseverance the race that is set before us, looking to Jesus the pioneer and perfecter of our faith, who for the joy that was set before him endured the cross, despising the shame, and is seated at the right hand of the throne of God." Notice the sequence: cross, shame, right hand. "Christ crucified" — those were Paul's words for it, but people never like to see those two words together. Christ helped the Christians to see that these highest expressions of power in the Messianic Psalms needed the deep humility and creativity of suffering in Isaiah 53 as a full commentary and both needed the Lord Jesus Christ in the incarnation to give them the thrust which has sent them to the center of history. Holy divinity and power are characterized here then as humble, self-sacrificing service that throws itself upon destructive evil with the utter self-abandon of the soldier who smothers with his own body a live grenade that has fallen among his buddies.

The New Testament writers have no hesitation in ripping these from their context in the Old Testament because they knew that they had the highest even of the Old Testament on their side as so convincingly confirmed in Christ. The New Testament writers were at the task of redeeming metaphors. While they were in the business of converting men, they were also converting a whole literature which reflects in its own way a form of double-mindedness that spoke of David being commanded by God to do battle and then denied the privilege of building the temple because his hands were bloody. Yet, we stand in the same place. We carry out the Word in one hand and a bomb in the other. That kind of thinking among Christians must go.

As Anabaptists, I think God has a special job

for us to do. Desperately needed in our own time is a vigorous reexamination of our own worldly power cultures as a monotonous repetition of the power culture of much of the Old Testament that weds the faith and the sword. Such reexamination must be done under the light of the cross and the radical obedience of the Son of God to the highest in the experience of the people Israel which He embodied. In the process of such reexamination certain basic issues will be encountered.

Faith is not minimized but understood in its full biblical sense. Eugene Nida, in a book that records the experiences of many translators of the Bible, says that there is a certain Indian tribe in Latin America that does not distinguish between "obedience" and "faith." [2] They cannot understand that our language has two different words for what they consider to be essentially the same thing; these they combine in one word. In the introduction to Paul's Epistle to the Romans he comes very close to identifying them when he speaks of the "obedience of faith."

Warfare and even race are regarded as firmly accepted in the Bible according to some Christians. To eliminate them may almost seem like opening the canon and making some changes. There is a sense in which the New Testament did just that for a tightly closed Old Testament canon. For in the perfect obedience of Christ it found a new fact to be incorporated in what had been given. Since Christ was anticipated in the Old Testament, the New Testament writers, of course, did not regard this as reopening the question of canon though it certainly appeared to be that to the Jews. While we expect no new fact to improve upon Christ and regard the question of canon as definitely closed, we may confidently expect that if Anabaptist Christians are faithful in interpreting Scripture from the standpoint of radical obedience certain approaches to biblical interpretation which make war at home in the New Testament will have to be set aside. One is worried that this may not be done soon enough when one sees many of the finest minds among Anabaptists being drawn into science where fulfillment is seen not in love and in persons but in the manipulation of things, where ultimate Messianic hope is seen in the one who has the most satellites in the skies instead of the One who has given His life in a sacrifice that gave the world salvation.

This does not mean the rejection of the Old Testament as some may think. Rather, it means accepting it as a living book where we find our own double-mindedness mirrored. I would recommend that we do not rationalize the tension by accepting excessive forms of dispensationalism or irreverent criticism, but that we see ourselves in its tension. There are still great denominations and some among our own people who feel there comes a time when it is right to take arms and kill. As a double-minded people the Old Testament "finds" us and leads us to Christ; it is truly the schoolmaster to faith. Furthermore, if we reject the Old Testament, it will be surely necessary for us to provide some counterpart for it. Sometimes I wonder if certain forms of psychology may not be an attempt on the part of man, particularly as they are applied to the religious realm, to give an adequate substitute for the Old Testament because of some of the problems that we encounter there. Modern literature or even our national histories have been used in this way. But is human experience in these anywhere nearly as broad or as theologically deep as that in the Old Testament?

Furthermore, if one turns to substitutes for the Old Testament, most of the New Testament becomes unintelligible since it consistently employs Old Testament terms. The Dutch scholar overstated the case when he said the New Testament is nothing but a glossary of Old Testament terms, but his point is sound. [3] Apply this, for example, to a term very central in the Scriptures — Christ. Paul epitomizes what Christ has done with "We preach Christ crucified." Now "Christ" is the Greek translation of Hebrew "Messiah" or "Anointed One," a term of far-reaching political and national significance.

"Messiah crucified" was to the Jews perfectly unthinkable and to the Greeks, foolishness; to too much of the Christian world today it is thoroughly objectionable, because these Christians cannot see how suffering and death can be power. And yet it was the step to the throne of power for the Master.

Growing out of all this is the fact that when the church was preaching the penetrating message of salvation for the hearts of men, it was crushing nationalism. That is amazing! They did not know when they were in social action; they did not know when they were in evangelism. They were working back and forth between them without even realizing when they crossed the line. The same spirit that purified the church at Pentecost drove race out of the apostolic church. How is it that we have so weakened evangelism by taking all the teeth out of it? The teeth are the very social, economic, political, the deeply personal problems of people; salvation is intimately related to every one of them. We are one whole. Christ came to save the whole of the individual man and the society. If we preach an evangelism that is concerned only about the ultimate salvation of souls and is not concerned about the body, the mind, the emotions, and the group, we are preaching only one fourth of a gospel. If we are preaching only one fourth of a gospel, perhaps we are preaching people out of the kingdom because we are not touching them at their basic needs. People are converted at the point of their most real need.

There is as much going on in the secular press by way of calling attention to some of these things as from our various pulpits. In a news item featured with a photograph *The Chicago Daily News* showed two veterans of World War II with battle flags before them. [4] These were flags that the Japanese soldiers carried on their person. They had been given to them ceremoniously at the time they left their home community. Many friends and relatives wrote wishes on these flags to these departing Japanese soldiers and then signed their names. They would carry these on their person right into battle. After they killed the Japanese, the Americans pulled these flags out of their clothes as souvenirs and took them back home. Now, the headline says, "Jap war flag haunts vet into returning souvenirs." Note how their consciences are bothering them. How can evangelists pass up the supreme opportunity of speaking to consciences heavy with guilt from war experiences? Let us not forget the resources of the New Testament evangelists who took bloody, nationalistic, yet soul-stirring battle songs that were deeply ingrained in the hearts of the people. They showed them that the true victor in every real battle is the Man on the cross who eliminates enemies not by shedding their blood but by allowing His own blood to be shed to reconcile man to God. Let us remember that to come into a worship service is to come into a throne room; that to join in the hymn is to engage in the coronation, following a mighty victory of the Lamb that was slain; that to offer our allegiance is to come to the only throne of ultimate power in the universe — a cross before an empty tomb.

Little wonder then, that it was once said of the Christians who were being tortured, "The amazing thing about Christians is that they sing while they suffer."

Christian Warfare

The Christian is imbued with the spirit of warfare if he models his life on that of his Lord. At the Nazareth synagogue Jesus, in a nine-word sermon-commentary on Isaiah 61:1, 2, asserted that the Spirit of the Lord was upon Him. This was Jesus' firm acceptance of Isaiah's rejection of physical might and warfare so repeatedly associated with the "Spirit of the Lord"; for the most numerous usage of the expression "Spirit of the Lord" in the Old Testament is in the Book of Judges. The expression is particularly associated with Samson in connection with physical brawn and action against Israel's enemy, the Philistines (Judges 13: 25; 14:6, 19; especially 15:14). Jesus' readiness to offer His own life as the fulfillment of the ancient prophecy was a living commentary that led to His being driven from His own hometown. This inaugural speech keynoted a life of conflict and rejection. "Today this Scripture has been fulfilled in your hearing" is the nine-word sermon equivalent to a declaration of independence from a whole institutional structure in which war was necessary. His action called (and calls) for His disciples likewise to offer their lives as the agonizing fulfillment of the ancient prophecy. This fulfillment involves giving to the word the flesh and blood of living, compassionately joyful obedience.

Because he has his own war to wage, the Christian breaks completely with the earthly strategy of physical combat. If the Christian is to be true to the Lord Jesus Christ, he must make a full break with the ancient and ultimate apostasy. His weaponry is not the belligerent word of ultimatum issuing in the thrust of the sword that divides, destroys, and perpetuates the very evil he is seeking to eliminate. His weaponry is rather the persuasive word of the gospel issuing in compassionate concern for liberation, reconciliation, and celebration of the approaching Christ-ordained age of peace.

From Jesus and the Scriptures by which he charters the course of his life, the Christian pacifist learn of a "Gulf Stream" within the larger turbulent ocean of history. The Christian is convinced of this because of the daring projection-confirmation (promise-fulfillment) pattern found in the Scriptures. The stream draws the openhearted, honest seeker into its mighty sweep as he commits his life to its mysterious though compelling flow which blesses and judges all history. From compassionate Joseph in the earliest strata of Old Testament literature through the Suffering Servant of Isaiah, and on through the quiet pacifist cosmogony of Genesis 1 and 2, one sees a mighty witness in mortal combat with Israel's national theology. On the cross of the Servant Lord, whose mission is predicted in Isaiah 53 and even framed in the language of holy war (verse 1, "arm of the Lord"; verse 12, "he shall divide the spoil with the strong"), the victory of implicit theological pacifism in the Old Testament prepares for incontrovertibly explicit pacifism in the New Testament.

The Christian pacifist is deeply conscious of strategy. Being deeply involved in history because of his commitment to Scripture, he knows the natural power of linked lives in service of selfishness whether personal or national. He is more deeply convinced of the Spirit-endowed power of suffering compassionate love to overcome and outstrip the shattering disintegrating force of antagonism and hatred. He believes profoundly that history, as someone has said in scoffing, "is news from a graveyard." Death itself is commandeered to accomplish ultimate pacification through the risen Lord of history.

The Christian pacifist is under no illusion about personal security as he follows Jesus. The safest place in conflict situations which overwhelm him is following Jesus closely and obediently. On the one hand, this means being caught in human misery, need, and trouble as he seeks to extend the gospel's compassionate embrace. On the other hand, as was true of Jesus, this way will set a man at odds with the "holy" who see his compassion for the sinner as a threat to the "purity" and hence the "effectiveness" of the establishment.

The Christian pacifist not only affirms the classic doctrines of incarnation and substitution. He sees in them an explication of his Word-weaponry strategy. The templehood of the individual Christian, as well as the body of Christians, is built on the model of Christ's inimitable work for man. The new age is the age of the beauty of human temples — Jesus and His circle of disciples include militarists, corrupt politicians, puzzled and errant theologians, as well as the sick of mind and body, who bring their hearts, battle-scarred by their struggle with indecision, pride, and pretense. And love — identifying, interceding, and interposing love — begins the process of personal and social pacification.

The Christian pacifist recognizes the power

of literature. He senses particularly the power of metaphor within the powerfully emotive and motivating form of poetry. From the figure of the "arm of the Lord" in Isaiah 53 to President Nixon's reference in his recent visit in China to "the long march" (called the "Exodus" of modern Chinese history) or "this is the hour" (of Chairman Mao), literary artists have used figures of speech to commandeer communication for purposes of engineering massive shift of viewpoint. In the Scriptures this received its highest pitch of daring by rewriting the nation-centered poetry. Taking the militaristic metaphor of a Messianic psalm, the Gospel writers use it as a headline for a completely pacifist news story about the Savior from sin who demonstrates how God deals with His enemies!

Footnotes

CHAPTER TWO

1. L. Finkelstein, ed., *The Jews: Their History, Culture, and Religion* (New York; 1950), p. xxi.

2. Oscar Cullmann, *Christ and Time,* tr. by Floyd V. Filson (Philadelphia: 1950), p. 17 f.; for the subsequent history of the calendar we are also indebted to this reference.

3. *Ibid.*, p. 18 n.

CHAPTER THREE

1. The word "Bible" is derived from the form of the Scriptures and means "books"; the Greek root means "papyrus."

2. *The Challenge of Israel's Faith* (Chicago: 1946), p. 77.

3. One should be cautioned against any tendency to be excessively critical about how much of this is from Moses' time. For we do know that the overall pattern (the recital of what God had done, the stipulations of God in commandment, the provisions for gifts to the temple, the curses and blessings for rebellion and disobedience, and the formal affirmation of allegiance ceremony) follows a typical pattern of treaty covenant common among the Hittites before the time of Moses. These covenant forms or treaty forms were intended to stabilize the Hittite empire. It was the arrangement initiated by the king with vassals. G. E. Mendenhall, "Covenant Forms in Israelite Tradition," *Biblical Archaeologist*, Vol. XVII (September 1954), pp. 57-60.

4. David Noel Freedman, "The Unity of the Bible," *Western Watch* (publication of Western Theological Seminary, Pittsburgh, Pennsylvania), Vol. VII (1956), p. 13.

CHAPTER FOUR

1. Cf. W. F. Albright, "What Were the Cherubim?" in the *Biblical Archaeologist*, Vol. 1, No. 1 (1938), pp. 1 f.

2. For an extended study of the Holy War in the Old Testament see Gerhard von Rad's monograph; *Der Heilige Krieg im Alten Israel*, Göttingen (1952). See also John W. Miller, "Holy War in the Old Testament," *Gospel Herald*, Vol. XLVIII, No. 11 (March 15, 1955).

3. See the writer's "The Book of Exodus as a Literary Type

for the Gospel of John," *Journal of Biblical Literature*, Vol. 76, No. 3 (1957), pp. 208-215.

4. Gordon D. Kaufman, "Nonresistance and Responsibility," *Concern*, No. 6 (November 1958, though circulated earlier).

CHAPTER FIVE

1. George Adam Smith, in his Lyman Beecher Lectures, *Modern Criticism and the Preaching of the Old Testament* (New York, 1901), p. 3, insists: "The Old Testament, one cannot too often remember, lies not *under* but behind the New Testament."

CHAPTER SIX

1. Cf. Donald G. Miller, *Fire in Thy Mouth* (New York, 1954), p. 44.

2. *God's Word in Man's Language* (New York, 1952), p. 121.

3. A. A. van Ruler, *Religie en Politiek*, quoted in Study 51E/125, May, 1951 (Geneva: Study Department, World Council of Churches), p. 7; also, Donald G. Miller, *op. cit.*, p. 44.

4. *Chicago Daily News* (July 22, 1957), p. 14.

The Author

Jacob J. Enz was born at Newton, Kansas. His early vocational training and involvement was with his father, an auto trimmer and canvas manufacturer. His formal schooling was at Bethel College, North Newton, Kansas; New York Theological Seminary; the Divinity School of the University of Chicago; he received his PhD from The Johns Hopkins University, Baltimore. He has done postdoctoral research at Harvard University in addition to research at Hebrew Union College, Jerusalem, being recipient of a Fulbright grant; he participated in archaeological digs at biblical Ashdod and Masada. Married to the former Joan Veston of New York, he is the father of two sons.

He served for four years as pastor of the First Mennonite Church, Nappanee, Indiana. He also served on the faculties of Goshen College, Goshen, Indiana, and Bethel College before coming to Mennonite Biblical Seminary, Elkhart, Indiana, in 1954 where he is currently Professor of Old Testament and Hebrew. He has served as editor of **The Mennonite** (1948-50) and has contributed to the **Journal of Biblical Literature.** In 1957 he was Menno Simons lecturer at Bethel College, the present work being the publication of these lectures.